Wyatt the Walrus
Makes a Friend

Written and Illustrated by Jacki Morariu

Wyatt the Walrus
Makes a New Friend

Written and Illustrated by Jacki Morariu

An AcuteByDesignBook

Published by AcuteByDesign

Text copyright © Jacki Morariu
Illustration copyright © Jacki Morariu

All rights reserved. No part of this publication can be reproduced, or transmitted in any form or by any means, electronic or mechancial, including photocopying, recording, or any inforamtion storage and retrieval system, without the prior written permission of the publisher.

ISBN: 978-1-943515-55-4

Published in United States By
AcuteByDesign
Marlborough, Connecticut

Dedicated to Sam for always believing in me, and seeing past my "tiny tusk"

Wyatt the walrus was different from others.

He didn't even look like his sisters or brothers.

His one tiny tusk
looked a little bit strange.
He wanted nothing more
than for that to change.

"You're great how you are!"
his mother would say.
But poor Wyatt was teased
almost every day.

HE KNEW HE WAS FUN
WITH *SO MUCH* LOVE TO GIVE

BUT THE MEAN WORDS FROM HIS PEERS
WERE HARD TO FORGIVE.

He wanted a friend!
He tried as hard as he could.
But poor Wyatt the walrus

was misunderstood.

He knew he looked different,
but his heart was the same.

If he couldn't make friends
his tusk must be to blame.

Since Wyatt the walrus had a tusk
that was short,
he heard walruses whisper
and laugh til they snort.

Even the humans
in a language unknown,
would giggle and point
and take pictures on their phone.

"JUST LEAVE ME ALONE,"
HE WOULD CRY EVERY DAY.

REALLY WISHING THAT SOMEONE
WOULD ASK HIM TO PLAY.

Then one day something happened he couldn't believe!

When he sat with the
new walrus
she didn't leave!

"Hi, I'm Wyatt," he said.
His voice starting to quake,

and he stuck out a flipper
waiting for her to shake.

She took it, and shook it,
her face in a smile.

The smile Wyatt returned
was his first in a while.

HE COULDN'T BELIEVE IT!
HE WAS MAKING A FRIEND!

HE HOPED THAT THIS MOMENT
WOULD NEVER END!

She said, "My name is Marie
my favorite color is blue!"

Wyatt was so excited!
That's his favorite too!

THEY KEPT TALKING AND TALKING,
IT WAS GOING SO WELL!
HE WAS MAKING A NEW FRIEND FOR LIFE
HE COULD JUST TELL!

THEY SPENT THE DAY LAUGHING
IT WAS SO MUCH FUN!
HE HATED LEAVING
WHEN THE DAY WAS DONE.

He woke up the next morning excited for class.
Not even noticing his tusk in the
mirrors he passed.

If Marie didn't care about it then
neither did he!
Wyatt's new confidence was easy to see.

What Marie liked about him
was his heart and his mind.
She said, "Good friends like you
are hard to find."

Now Wyatt had a friend
even with a tusk that's too small.
Marie didn't care about it,
not one bit, not at all.

Other kids started to notice
the two friends at play.
They were having more
and more fun, everyday!

One by one all the classmates
asked to join in.
Wyatt was happy to include them
with a great big grin.

Now Wyatt has more friends
than he thought that he could.

He felt loved, he felt happy,
and he felt understood.

THE MORAL OF THIS STORY
IS WHEN YOU MEET SOMEONE NEW,
IF YOU'RE A WALRUS, A CROCODILE,
OR A KANGAROO,

NO MATTER WHAT
ALWAYS BE WHO YOU ARE!
AND OTHERS WILL SEE
YOU ARE TRULY A STAR!

Made in the USA
Middletown, DE
18 October 2022